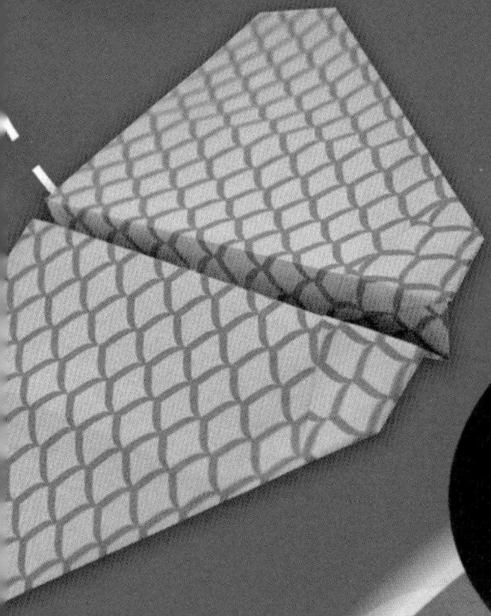

Air-igami

ORIGAMI GLIDERS

CATHERINE ARD

PowerKiDS
press™

Published in 2019 by
The Rosen Publishing Group, Inc.
29 East 21st Street, New York, NY 10010

Cataloging-in-Publication Data

Names: Ard, Catherine.
Title: Origami gliders / Catherine Ard.
Description: New York : PowerKids Press, 2019. | Series: Air-ogami | Includes glossary and index.
Identifiers: ISBN 9781538347089 (pbk.) | ISBN 9781538347102 (library bound) | ISBN 9781538347096 (6pack)
Subjects: LCSH: Origami–Juvenile literature. | Gliders (Aeronautics)–Models–Juvenile literature.
Classification: LCC TT872.5 A733 2019 | DDC 736'.982–dc23

Models and photography: Michael Wiles
Text: Catherine Ard
Design: Picnic, with Emma Randall
Edited: Kate Overy, with Julia Adams

Manufactured in the United States of America

CPSIA Compliance Information: Batch #CWPK19:
For Further Information contact
Rosen Publishing, New York, New York
at 1-800-237-9932.

# Contents

Basic folds

This book shows you how to make a fantastic fleet of paper gliders. All you need for each amazing model is a sheet of paper, your fingers, and some clever creasing. So, get folding and get flying!

GETTING STARTED

The paper we've used for these aircraft is thin, but strong, so that it can be folded many times. You can use ordinary scrap paper, but make sure it's not too thick.

A lot of the gliders in this book are made with the same folds. The ones that appear most are explained on these pages. It's a good idea to try out these folds before you start.

KEY

When making the gliders, follow this key to find out what the lines, arrows, and symbols mean.

·   mountain fold

↷   direction to move paper

– – – – – – – – – – –   valley fold

◀ ▶   direction to push or pull paper

MOUNTAIN FOLD

To make a mountain fold, fold the paper so that the crease is pointing up at you, like a mountain.

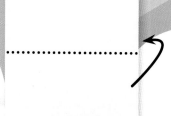

VALLEY FOLD

To make a valley fold, fold the paper the other way, so that the crease is pointing away from you, like a valley.

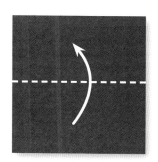

OUTSIDE REVERSE FOLD

An outside reverse fold can be used to create an aircraft's nose.

1 First try folding a piece of paper diagonally. Make a valley fold on one point and crease.

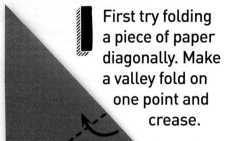

2 It's important to make sure that the paper is creased well. Run your finger over the crease two or three times.

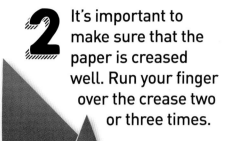

3 Unfold and open up the corner slightly. Refold the crease farthest away from you into a valley fold.

4 Open up the paper a little more and start to turn the corner inside out. Then close the paper when the fold begins to turn.

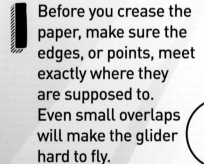

5 OPEN

You now have an outside reverse fold. You can either flatten the paper or leave it rounded out.

FOLDING TIPS

Paper aircraft are easy to make, and fun to fly, but you need to fold with care if your creations are going to glide, loop, twirl, and dive the way they are meant to.

1 Before you crease the paper, make sure the edges, or points, meet exactly where they are supposed to. Even small overlaps will make the glider hard to fly.

2 Use a ruler to help you line up your creases, especially when you are folding a sharp nose point, or creasing several layers of paper at once.

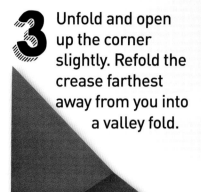

USE A RULER!

3 The left side of the aircraft is always a mirror image of the right side. Carefully line up the second wing to match the first wing.

4 Before you fly a glider, check that the wings and wing tips are sitting at the same angle on each side. Crooked wings won't fly!

Storm Surfer

Fold this dazzling zigzag glider to streak through the sky like a bolt from the blue. It's so simple, it will be ready in a flash!

FLASH AND DASH!

FLIP OVER

6 MORE TO GO!

1 Place the paper as shown. Fold over the top a finger's width from the edge.

2 Continue to fold over six more times, keeping the folds even.

3 Turn the paper over.

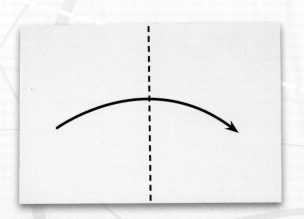

4 Fold the paper in half from left to right.

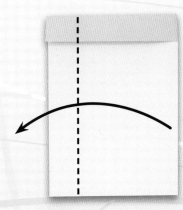

5 Fold back the top layer to make the first wing.

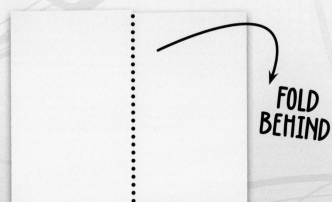

FOLD
BEHIND

6 Mountain fold the right side, lining it up with the wing you just made.

OPEN UP

7 Pinch the paper underneath and pull up the wings.

8 Hold the paper just behind the folded edge. Aim slightly upward and gently throw to let your glider surf and then softly land!

FINISHED!

Super Swooper

This wide-winged flier will not disappoint. Aim it high above your head and throw. Watch it glide and twist to land. Amazing!

DUCK AND DIVE!

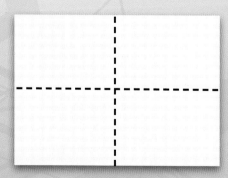

1 Place the paper as shown. Fold it in half from left to right and unfold, then from top to bottom and unfold.

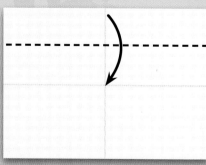

2 Valley fold the top edge to meet exactly on the center crease.

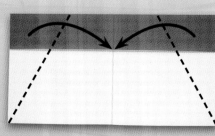

3 Fold in the corners so that the top edges meet on the center crease.

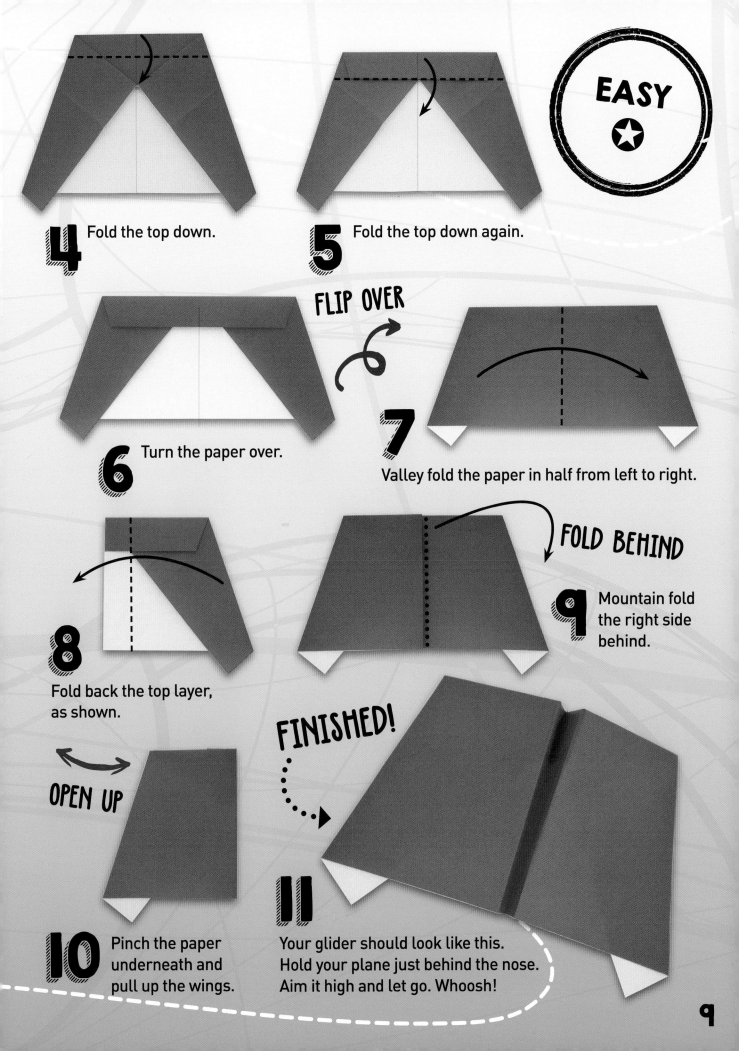

4 Fold the top down.

5 Fold the top down again.

EASY ★

6 Turn the paper over.

FLIP OVER

7 Valley fold the paper in half from left to right.

8 Fold back the top layer, as shown.

FOLD BEHIND

9 Mountain fold the right side behind.

OPEN UP

FINISHED!

10 Pinch the paper underneath and pull up the wings.

11 Your glider should look like this. Hold your plane just behind the nose. Aim it high and let go. Whoosh!

Blue Condor

Wow your friends with this winged wonder. Watch it silently soar, then glide on the wind before sweeping back to Earth.

RIDE AND GLIDE!

1 Place the paper as shown. Fold it in half from left to right and unfold.

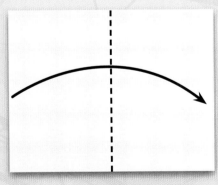

2 Fold the top corners so that the points meet halfway down the center crease.

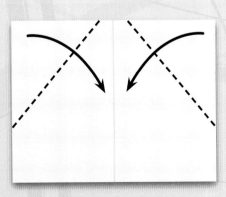

3 Make two angled folds on the top edge, as shown.

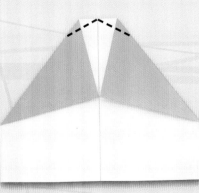

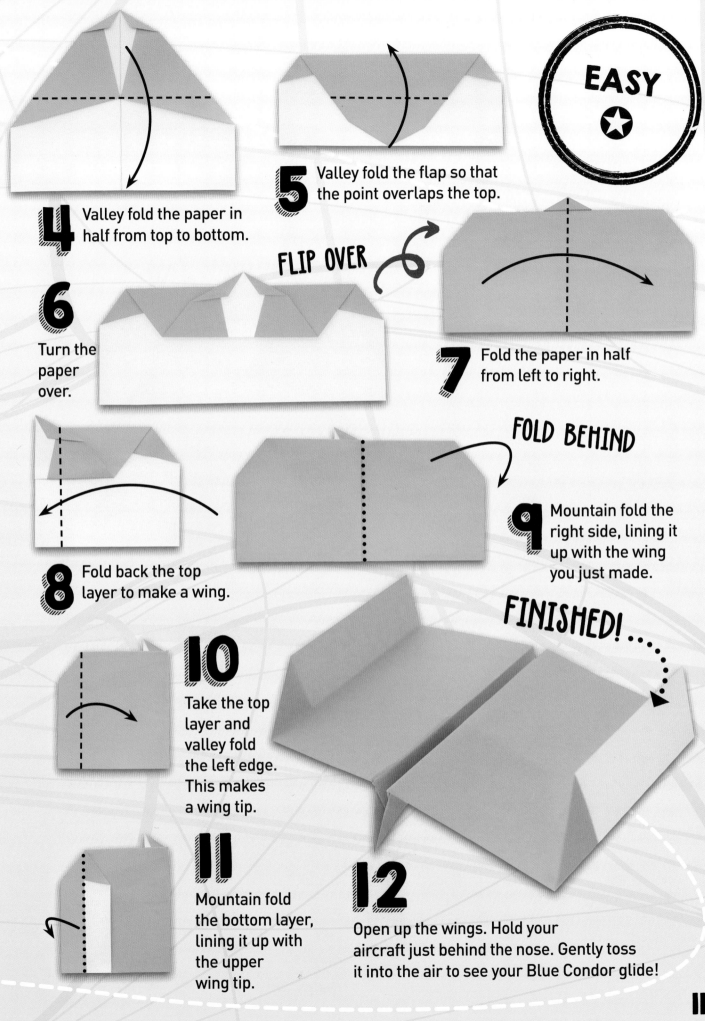

4 Valley fold the paper in half from top to bottom.

5 Valley fold the flap so that the point overlaps the top.

FLIP OVER

6 Turn the paper over.

7 Fold the paper in half from left to right.

FOLD BEHIND

8 Fold back the top layer to make a wing.

9 Mountain fold the right side, lining it up with the wing you just made.

FINISHED!

10 Take the top layer and valley fold the left edge. This makes a wing tip.

11 Mountain fold the bottom layer, lining it up with the upper wing tip.

12 Open up the wings. Hold your aircraft just behind the nose. Gently toss it into the air to see your Blue Condor glide!

Pterosaur

Take some gliding tips from fearsome early fliers. With its pointy prehistoric shape, this super soarer could be straight out of the Jurassic jungle!

SWOOP AND SOAR!

OPEN UP

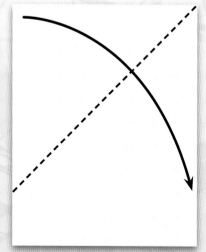

1 Place the paper as shown. Valley fold the top edge to meet the right-hand edge.

2 Open up the paper.

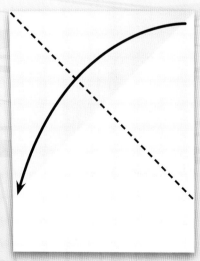

3 Now valley fold the top edge to meet the left-hand edge.

FLIP OVER

 Open up the paper.

 You should have a creased cross. Turn the paper over.

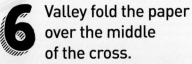 Valley fold the paper over the middle of the cross.

 Open up the paper.

 Turn the paper over.

FLIP OVER

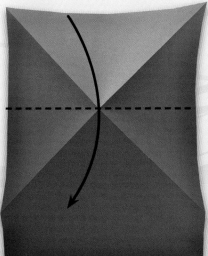

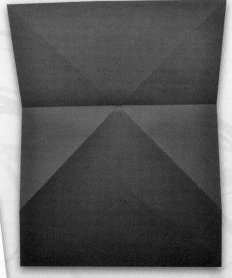

PUSH IN HERE
▼

 Push in on the center point to make the sides pop up.

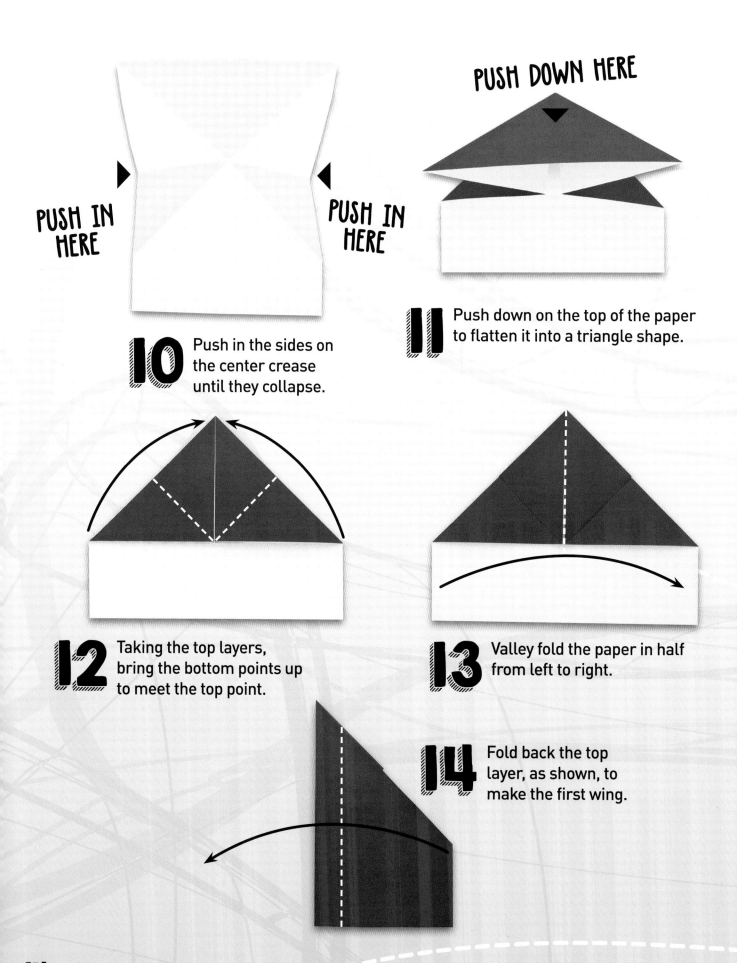

PUSH IN HERE

PUSH IN HERE

PUSH DOWN HERE

10 Push in the sides on the center crease until they collapse.

11 Push down on the top of the paper to flatten it into a triangle shape.

12 Taking the top layers, bring the bottom points up to meet the top point.

13 Valley fold the paper in half from left to right.

14 Fold back the top layer, as shown, to make the first wing.

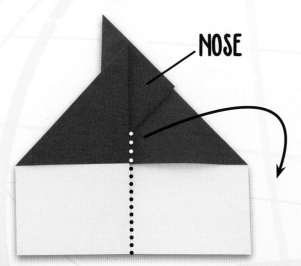

NOSE

15 Mountain fold the right side, lining it up with the wing you just made. Don't fold the triangular nose.

16 Take the top layer and valley fold the left edge. This makes a wing tip.

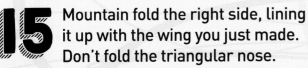

17 Mountain fold the bottom layer, lining it up exactly with the upper wing tip.

18 Pinch the paper underneath and open up the wings. Make sure they are level.

FOLD BEHIND

OPEN UP ⇄

...FINISHED!

19 Straighten the wing tips. Hold the glider underneath and throw it gently forward to send your Pterosaur soaring!

Jungle Hawk

Go undercover with this stealthy glider! Take it to a park or field and you can send it sailing, unseen, among the trees!

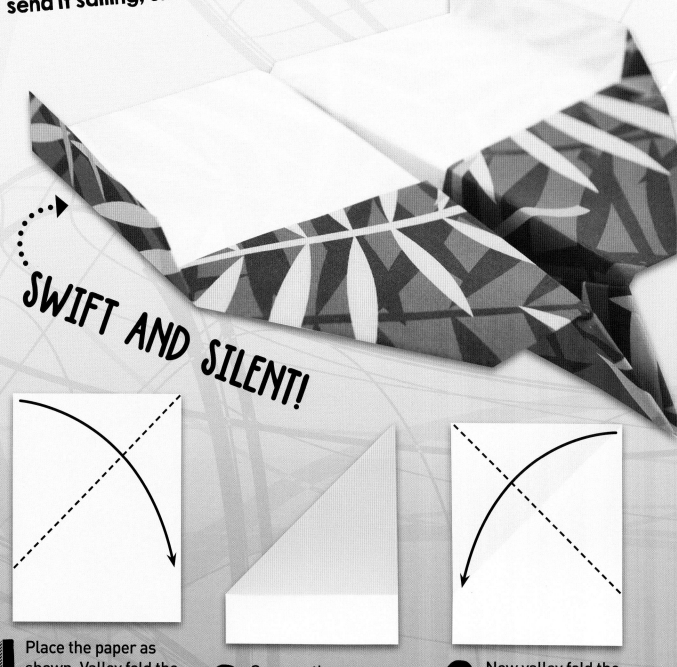

SWIFT AND SILENT!

1 Place the paper as shown. Valley fold the top edge to meet the right-hand edge.

2 Open up the paper.

3 Now valley fold the top edge to meet the left-hand edge.

OPEN UP

FLIP OVER

4 Open up the paper.

5 You should have a creased cross. Turn the paper over.

6 Valley fold the paper over the middle of the cross.

7 Open up the paper once more.

8 Turn the paper over.

FLIP OVER

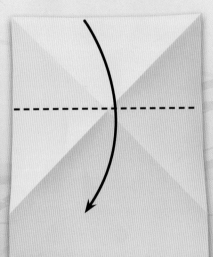

PUSH IN HERE
▼

9 Push in on the center point to make the sides pop up.

PUSH IN HERE ▶

◀ PUSH IN HERE

11 Push down on the top of the paper to flatten it into a triangle shape.

10 Push in the sides on the center crease until they collapse.

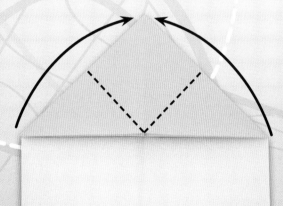

12 Taking the top layers, bring the bottom points up to meet the top point. This makes a square.

13 Fold the bottom left edge of the square to meet the center crease.

14 Open out the fold you just made.

15 Now fold the top left edge of the square to meet the center crease.

16 Open out the fold you just made.

17 Now repeat on the other side. Fold the bottom right edge of the square to meet the center crease.

18 Open out the fold you just made.

19 Fold the top right edge of the square to meet the center crease.

20 Open out the fold you just made.

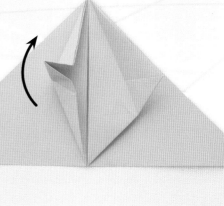

21 Your paper should look like this.

22 On the left side, pinch the corner and fold in along the creases.

23 Flatten the paper to make a triangular flap.

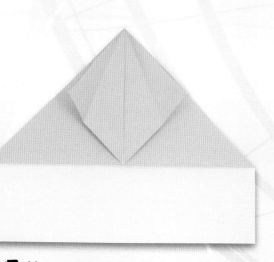

24 Repeat on the other side. Pinch the corner and fold in to make a triangular flap.

FOLD BEHIND

25 Mountain fold the point. Leave the flaps you just made sticking out at the top.

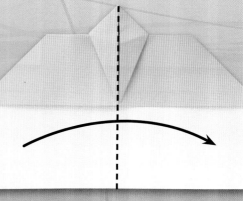

26 Fold the paper in half from left to right.

27 Valley fold the top layer, as shown. This makes the first wing.

28 Mountain fold the other side, lining it up with the wing you just made.

FOLD BEHIND

29 Take the top layer and fold in the left-hand edge to make a wing tip.

30 Mountain fold the bottom layer, lining it up with the upper wing tip.

31 Pinch the paper underneath and open up the wings. Check that they are level.

OPEN UP

32 Straighten the wing tips and you are ready for takeoff. Aim high and toss it into the air!

FINISHED!

Sky Ray

Fold this great-winged glider right and it will sweep gracefully through the blue, just like a manta ray cruising through the ocean!

SWEEP AND SWERVE!

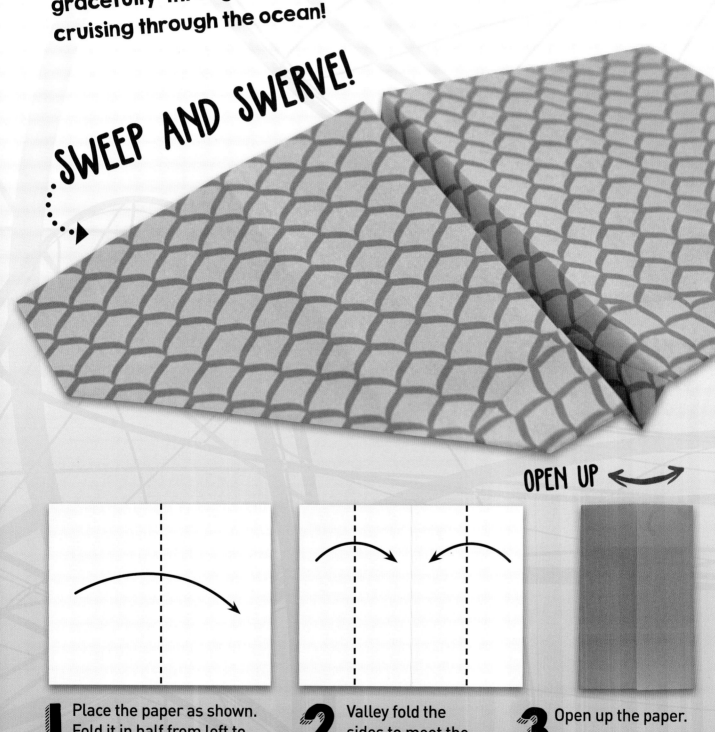

OPEN UP

1 Place the paper as shown. Fold it in half from left to right and unfold.

2 Valley fold the sides to meet the center crease.

3 Open up the paper.

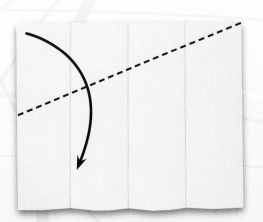

OPEN UP

4 Valley fold the top left corner to meet the first crease in from the left.

5 Open up the paper.

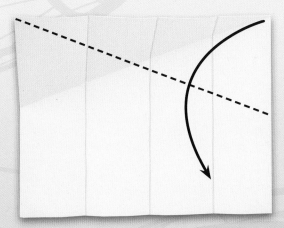

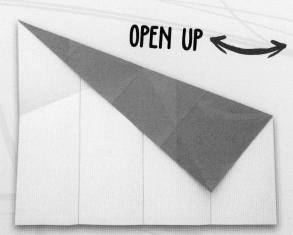

OPEN UP

6 Repeat on the other side. Fold the top right corner to meet the first crease in from the right.

7 Open up the paper.

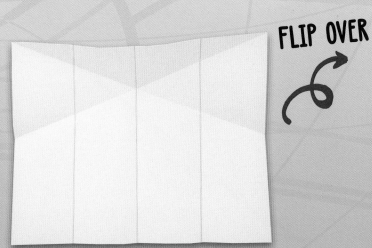

FLIP OVER

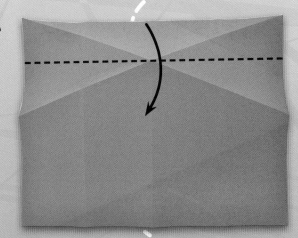

8 You should now have a creased cross. Turn the paper over.

9 Valley fold the top edge over the middle of the cross.

10 Open up the paper once more.

11 Turn the paper over.

12 Push in the sides on the center crease until they collapse.

PUSH DOWN HERE

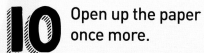

13 Push down on the top of the paper to flatten it into a wide triangle.

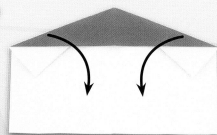

14 Fold down the flaps on either side.

15 Turn the paper over.

16 Valley fold the top point, as shown.

17 Turn the paper over.

18 Fold in the sides along the creases you made earlier.

FLIP OVER

19 Turn the paper over.

20 Valley fold the paper in half from right to left.

FOLD BEHIND

21 Take the top layer and fold it back to make the first wing.

22 Mountain fold the left side, lining it up with the wing you just made.

OPEN UP

FINISHED!

23

Pinch the paper underneath and open out the wings. Make sure they are level.

24 Hold your glider near the nose and gently toss it up to see it drift and dive!

Wind Rider

Prepare to be blown away by this easy-to-fold flyer! Catch the wind right, and watch it breeze effortlessly through the air.

SKIP AND SKIM!

1 Place the paper with the patterned side facing up. Fold it in half from top to bottom.

2 Take the top layer and fold up the edge to fall ½ inch (15 mm) from the top.

3 Fold over the top edge, as shown.

4 Valley fold the top corners to meet the edge of the flap.

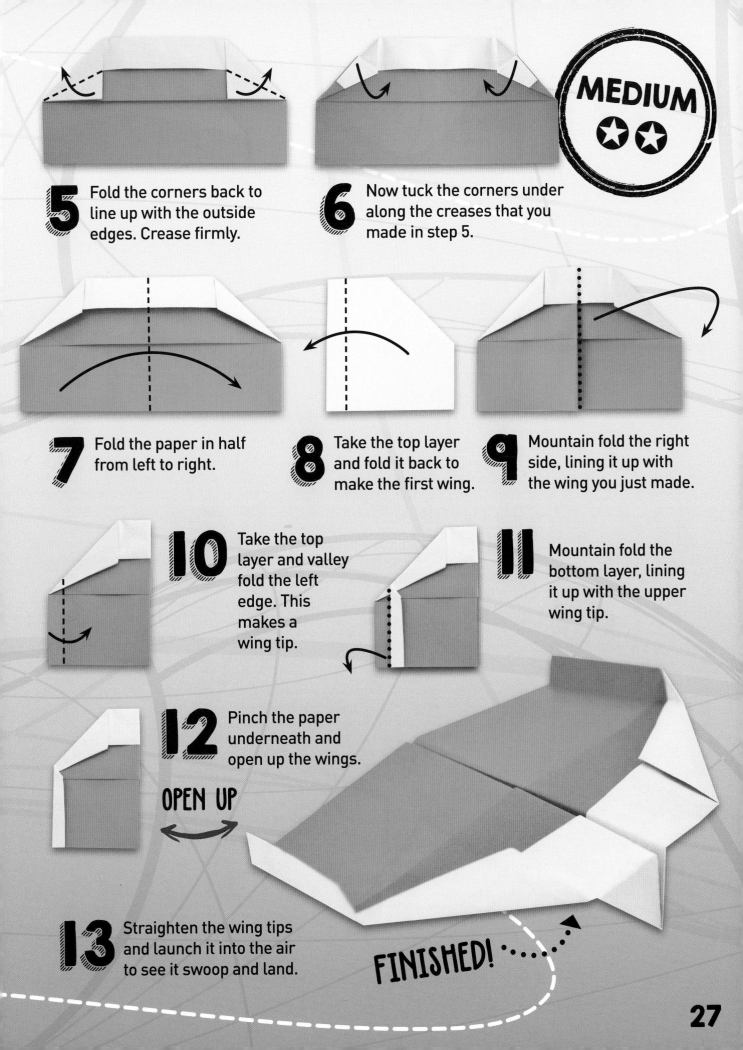

5 Fold the corners back to line up with the outside edges. Crease firmly.

6 Now tuck the corners under along the creases that you made in step 5.

7 Fold the paper in half from left to right.

8 Take the top layer and fold it back to make the first wing.

9 Mountain fold the right side, lining it up with the wing you just made.

10 Take the top layer and valley fold the left edge. This makes a wing tip.

11 Mountain fold the bottom layer, lining it up with the upper wing tip.

12 Pinch the paper underneath and open up the wings.

OPEN UP

13 Straighten the wing tips and launch it into the air to see it swoop and land.

FINISHED!

Pocket Glider

This small but nifty glider makes use of an air pocket to drift through the air.

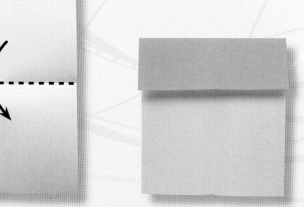

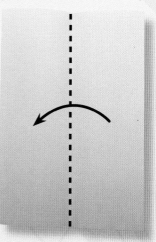

1 Place your paper so that it is portrait. Fold it from left to right down the center line, then unfold it again.

2 Now fold the paper in half from top to bottom, then unfold it. You have created a center cross where the creases meet.

3 Fold the top edge of the paper downward so the edge meets the center crease line that you created in step 2.

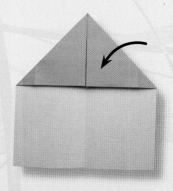

4 Now fold the top left-hand corner into the center crease, making sure the edge aligns with it perfectly.

5 Repeat step 4 on the right-hand corner. Both corners should align along the center crease.

6 Fold the top point downward, stopping a short way from the bottom edge, as shown.

7 Now fold the bottom point upward to align with the top straight edge of the paper. The point should fall directly in the center crease.

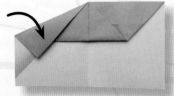
OPEN UP

8 Carefully fold in the top left-hand corner so that the top edge of your paper aligns with the center crease. Unfold this.

9 Now, make another fold inward so that the top edge of your paper aligns with the fold you created in step 8. Unfold this.

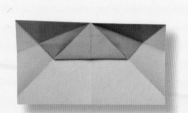

TUCK!

10 Repeat steps 8 and 9 on the top right-hand corner.

11 Finally, fold the top left-hand corner again, but this time push the corner under the central pocket that has formed. It helps to pull this pocket outward while you press the corner under. The remaining paper should fall diagonally from the center of the pocket out toward the wing edge.

12 Repeat step 11 on the right-hand corner, then turn the plane over.

FINISHED!

13 Press all your creases firmly and launch your glider by holding on to the pocket!

Glossary

bolt
A jagged flash of lightning.

condor
A South American vulture that soars above the Andes with the help of its huge wingspan.

fleet
A group of aircraft that fly together.

Jurassic
A prehistoric period during which dinosaurs roamed the Earth.

manta ray
A marine animal that has wide, flat side fins and a slim tail.

pterosaur
A flying reptile that was alive during the Jurassic and Cretaceous periods.

skim
To move lightly over or across something.

soar
To fly or rise very high in the air.

stealthy
To do something in a way that makes it barely noticeable.

streak
To move incredibly fast in one direction.

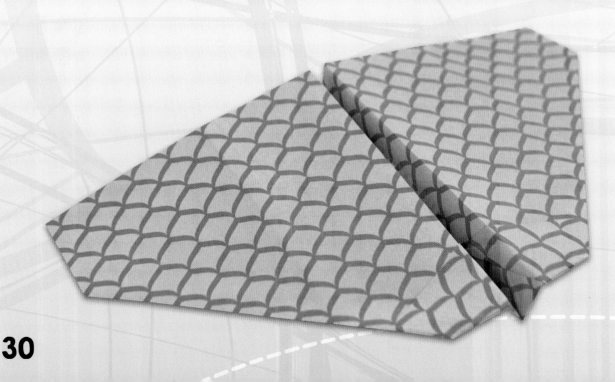

Further Information

Books:

Bounford, Trevor. *Build Your Own Paper Air Force*. London, UK: Ilex Press, 2010.

Boursin, Didier. *Origami Paper Airplanes*. Richmond Hill, Canada: Firefly, 2001.

Stillinger, Doug. *Book of Paper Airplanes*. New York, NY: Klutz, 2004.

Tudor, Andy. *100 More Paper Planes to Fold and Fly*. London, UK: Usborne, 2012.

Woodroffe, David. *The Complete Paper Aeroplane Book*. London, UK: Constable and Co, 2013.

Websites:

www.scienceforkidsclub.com/paper-airplanes.html
Visit this website to find out all about the science behind paper planes and what makes them fly faster and further.

https://www.youtube.com/watch?v=9jq-K8s7lnk
A video that shows you how to fold a windproof glider!

Publisher's note to educators and parents: Our editors have carefully reviewed these websites to ensure that they are suitable for students. Many websites change frequently, however, and we cannot guarantee that a site's future contents will continue to meet our high standards of quality and educational value. Be advised that students should be closely supervised whenever they access the Internet.

Index